HAPPY LANDING

JOSEPH D. PACE

iUniverse, Inc.
New York   Bloomington

iUniverse books may be ordered through booksellers or by contacting:

iUniverse
1663 Liberty Drive
Bloomington, IN 47403
www.iuniverse.com
1-800-Authors (1-800-288-4677)

Because of the dynamic nature of the Internet, any Web addresses or links contained in this book may have changed since publication and may no longer be valid. The views expressed in this work are solely those of the author and do not necessarily reflect the views of the publisher, and the publisher hereby disclaims any responsibility for them.

ISBN: 978-1-4401-4373-1 (sc)
ISBN: 978-1-4401-4374-8 (ebook)

Printed in the United States of America

iUniverse rev. date: 7/01/2009

To my wife Thelma, our daughter Carmela, our son Jonathan and all of our grandchildren, and in honor of all those who served in World War II.

ACKNOWLEDGEMENTS

Information was gleaned from Pilot Lt. Gerald D. White's log, Co-Pilot Lt. R. Peyton Woodson III's memory of events, and "The Snetterton Falcons II, The 96th Bomb Group in World War II" by Robert E. Doherty and Geoffrey D. Ward, English Contact/ Historian. I also would be remiss if I did not acknowledge the assistance of my wife, Thelma, who has faithfully made suggestions and done the typing in putting my story together.

CONTENTS

PREFACE

World War II was a very emotional experience for the young men, and even some women, actually still boys for the most part ranging in age from their late teens to early twenties, who fought so valiantly for their country. Whether the person was serving in the Army, Navy, Air Force, Marines or Merchant Marines, whether they were active on the ground, on the sea or in the air, each person has a story that could and should be told. Thus, there are thousands of stories out there. And mine is just one of those.

I had never considered writing my story or, for that matter, I really didn't even talk about my wartime experiences until I attended a reunion of the 96th Bomb Group with the "Mighty Eighth Air Force" at the Riviera Hotel in Las Vegas, Nevada, in 1990. While there, these men with whom I'd fought were telling of their experiences and asking about mine. We exchanged reminiscences, and the larger picture of this war started becoming clearer, identifying our individual roles in it and seeing how they meshed together to bring about the victory that was won. During subsequent reunions, we have all been encouraged to tell our individual stories so the people of this generation and succeeding generations can have a better understanding of what it takes to guarantee the freedoms this country enjoys.

The world had never seen combat like that of World War II,

and I prayed it never would again. But, unfortunately, as I attempt to put the finishing touches on my story of that war, our country is again at war, fighting in Afghanistan and Iraq against another enemy in a war against terrorism. Our country has again been attacked, something we had come to consider unthinkable. Again, our country's young people are fighting valiantly to defend against the evils of the world, and sadly, some are giving their lives in the quest, just as did so many of our generation in what we'd hoped to be the war to end all wars.

Having achieved my 88th birthday on November 1, 2008, it is imperative that I finish writing this story of my own part in that war, how I became involved in it and how I survived a forced parachute jump as our plane went down and my having landed in a German mine field. What I tell you is factual, these events actually happened, and I remember them as if it were yesterday.

IMMIGRANT ROOTS

My parents, Onofrio and Carmela Pace, grew up in the region of Bari in Italy. During the first year of their marriage and my mother being pregnant with their first child, my father's father gave him money and urged him to migrate to the United States to carve out a better life for his family. It was1920 and they traveled from Palo Del Colle, Bari, Italy to France, and sailed from the port of LeHavre on the S.S. Lafayette. Traveling in steerage, it was an arduous journey for this young couple, he being 19 years of age and she having attained her 20th birthday. They arrived at Ellis Island, New York City, on August 23, 1920.

A curious incident took place when my parents came through Ellis Island. My mother was held back after my father had already passed through while the doctor checked further to determine if her eyes were diseased. Turned out it was only a matter of a cold having settled in her eyes during the trip. In the meantime, my father was nervously waiting outside the building on a curb next to another immigrant (a German) who was about to eat a banana. The German immigrant motioned to ask if he would like a banana. My father accepted the offer, looked at the banana and not knowing how to eat it, bit into the banana, peel and all. The German motioned "no" and showed him how to peel and eat the banana.

They lived temporarily with my mother's sister Isabella and

her husband Louis Adinolfi, in New York City, who had previously migrated to the United States. And on November 1, 1920, I was born in my aunt's bed.

My father soon found work delivering ice and they established a home of their own in an apartment on East 117th Street, also in New York City. The family grew with the addition of two brothers, Dominick and Angelo, and then my sister Mary, born January 9, 1925, and another brother, Onofrio Joseph, born April 3, 1926.

In later years, my mother became very ill and the doctor advised my father to get out of the city. We moved to a rented house on 217th Street in the Upper Bronx, New York. In 1927, it was country. Later my parents purchased a two-story house on 219th Street.

We grew up in a predominantly Italian neighborhood and engaged in the typical city childhood games, such as "stickball" in the streets.

My father's sister Madelyn and her husband Frank Antezzo lived in an apartment in the Bronx, and there were frequent family gatherings. I recall helping my father make wine in our basement and my cousin would help his father make wine in the basement of his father's ice business. They'd compare their wines at our family dinners. Once when I was visiting my cousin, my uncle Frank gave me a gallon of his wine to take back to my father. It was in a brown paper sack. As I was riding the subway home it apparently received too much jostling and suddenly exploded, spilling the wine all over my clothing. As you can imagine, I was embarrassed to no end.

At an early age I went to a Catholic parochial school, public school, PS21 in the Bronx, and on to Evander Childs High School in the Upper Bronx, New York, where I graduated in 1936.

My mother had hoped I would continue with a college education and had visions of my becoming a doctor. However, my brothers, sister and I grew up during the "Great Depression" that began in 1928 and lasted into the 1930s. My father lost his small produce business, which put us on welfare. Being the oldest, I was called on to help support the family.

With jobs being extremely scarce, I went to work through the WPA (Work Project Administration) that President Roosevelt established and, later on, the National Youth Administration. I was assigned to Ellis Island as a clerk reviewing applications in preparation for U.S. citizenship, correction of information, spelling, dates, and checking the ships' logs to find petitioner's date of entry into the United States. A year or so later I finally landed a good job working for a large printing firm, J. J. Little and Ives, in New York City, earning $20 per week.

The Specter of War Looms

Adolf Hitler became chancellor of Germany on January 30, 1930. He had a long term goal of creating an empire taking back all of the territory Germany lost in World War I and more. This empire was to become what he deemed racially pure which would exclude those he considered inferior such as Jews, Slavs, gypsies and others. In order to accomplish his goals, he renounced the restrictions that had been placed on Germany's rearmament that resulted at the end of World War I and embarked on a rapid buildup of his armed forces. It was not long until he had a war machine in place that intimidated rival European powers. Italy's leader, Benito Mussolini became aligned with Hitler. Hitler's influence extended into Asia with Japan siding in with Hitler's Germany. When Germany invaded Poland on September 1, 1939, it marked the beginning of the war between the Axis and the Allies and in early 1942, America is building up to counter Germany in Europe and Japan in Asia. The U.S. Eighth Air Corps is created. The Mission: The strategic bombing of Nazi Germany.

Japan Strikes Pearl Harbor

I was 21 years old and enjoying a movie when news flashed across the screen that the Japanese attacked Pearl Harbor on December 7, 1941 in the Hawaiian Islands. Ironically, a flight of B-17s were due from California that morning, so the initial blips on the radar did not appear as a potential attack allowing the Japanese to take the Island of Oahu completely by surprise. In less than two hours 18 warships had been sunk or crippled. Additionally 188 planes were destroyed and 159 damaged. More than 2400 Americans were killed and nearly 1200 were wounded. The very next day President Franklin Delano Roosevelt made his declaration of war address to Congress using the phrase "a date which will live in infamy" in referring to this event. Not long thereafter my patriotic emotions demanded that I do my part, so February 18, 1942, I enlisted in the army and was inducted at Ft. Dix, New Jersey.

Two of my brothers also joined the armed services, Onofrio, who we called Babe, with the Navy, serving in the South Pacific, and Dominick with the Infantry, serving in Alaska. My brother Angelo did not serve due to impaired hearing resulting from a truck accident when he was a child.

I'M IN THE ARMY NOW

I asked for tank corps but, instead, I found myself on a troop train speeding down the tracks to Camp Croft, South Carolina. "What's there?" I wondered. And in talking with other recruits I discovered it was an infantry training camp, and not to my liking. I lamented to myself that I would go through the infantry training. I succeeded in becoming an expert BAR (Browning Automatic Rifleman) gunner, and received a rank of Private First Class (P.F.C.). I envisioned what would probably happen to me as a BAR gunner. Along with two ammo carriers, I probably would be killed on the first combat mission. The German fighters looked at any automatic weapons as a prime target.

Upon completion of the infantry training we were shipped by train to Ft. Devens, Massachusetts, as replacements where the 45th Infantry Division, The Thunderbirds, who made history during WWI, was stationed. The Division was a tough outfit, fully ready, and soon to be shipped out for combat duty in Africa. We recruits were to enhance the division. The first evening we were there, Captain Dunn had us stand roll call and made the statement that he realized we were all from the East, and he commented that we were degrading the unit. The unit had consisted of recruits from Oklahoma and New Mexico and many Indians. His comment did not set well with me; I thought we were all fighting this war together. Two others and I decided that we would get out of this outfit even at the risk of going over the captain's authority.

Late one night we were awakened with "Force march -- full pack, get ready." As I recall it was close to midnight and we walked for miles to the shores of the Atlantic Ocean. We were loaded on amphibious landing crafts and taken about 3 miles out and turned towards the shore to practice "invasion." Our scout jumped out first and immediately went under. We pulled him in and yelled, "Go further in!" And they took us in further. The gate dropped and, in charging, I hit a small sand dune, tripped and went head over heels with my BAR gun with sand flying about. I was glad it was practice and not actual combat.

ARMY AIR CORPS

The 45th Wing, 8th Air Force, the 96th Bomb Group (H) was constituted on the 28th of January 1942 in a War Department letter 320.2 from the Adjutant General. Lt. Colonel Hap Arnold was to lead the 96th Bomb Group (H). Many groups moved from place to place in the United States to be organized. Many airmen and B-17s and B-24s went through extensive training sessions in preparation for combat. Finally, all administrations, crews and pilots, airmen and ground personnel were shipped to England; ready for action.

The 96th Bomb Group (H) consisted of four squadrons, the 337th, 338th, 339th and the 413th, with a total of approximately 60 B-17s and operated from Eccles Road, Snetterton Heath, England, as the "Snetterton Falcons."

The 8th Air Corps, to be the largest air striking force ever committed to battle, operated entirely from the United Kingdom from over 100 bases.

On the most dangerous missions more than a quarter of American bombers failed to return. Ten hours of oxygen, intense cold, deafening noise, constant vibration, and a one-in-three chance of completing their tour of 25 missions were the average prospects for the crews. During WWII it was said there were no atheists in foxholes. You can be assured there were no atheists in the air either. We felt God's presence in many ways and knew He saved many lives.

The Army Air Corps was located adjacent to the 45th Infantry Division which made it easy for my two buddies and me to leave the area and apply for the Air Corps. Fascinated with the idea of flying an airplane, we crossed over to the Air Corps base and met with a sergeant. He asked us why we wanted to be in the Air Corps and we replied that we wanted to be fighter pilots. He responded, "Great, we need fighter pilots." We qualified but needed to return the next day to meet with the colonel for approval. However, when we returned to the base of the 45th, Captain Dunn was quite angry that we'd left the base without permission and restricted us to company area. Now, what to do; we talked it over and decided we'd just go anyway. So, next day we met with the colonel who gave us a 72-hour pass, told us to go see our girlfriends, wives, whatever, and report back to the Air Corps. We questioned about our belongings at the base of the 45th and he said not to go back there, things would be taken care of for us. Thus we managed a transfer to the Army Air Corps in November of 1942. Having passed the written tests and physicals, we became Army Air Corps Cadets to train as pilots. We were all shipped to different air fields and never saw one another again.

Joe Pace, an Army Air Corps Cadet in 1942

Pilot Training

In January of 1943, I was transferred to Corsicana, Texas, for Primary training where we flew the PT-19A – Fairchild. Halfway through training my instructor ordered me to land the aircraft. When I landed, the instructor got out, stood and looked up to me and said, "Kill yourself; you're not going to kill me." I guess he thought I was flying like a hot pursuit pilot. That's when I soloed. I loved flying this aircraft. Acted like a fighter. At times during solo flying I would fly up to an altitude of 2,000 feet and then place the aircraft into a spinning dive and see how close I could get to the ground before pulling up out of the dive. I found this thrilling. Looking back, I realize it really was not a bright stunt.

This was followed by basic training at Greenville, Texas, flying the BT-13A, Valiant. Unfortunately, I had a bad experience and after a check flight, my instructor told me it was possible that I could fly, but "there's a war on and pilots are needed fast" and that he did not have the time to teach me. So, April of '43 found me "washed-out", grounded, much to my chagrin.

138

P.T. 19-A   "FAIRCHILD".

CONSOLIDATED-VULTEE BT-13A 'VALIANT'

WASHED OUT - NOW WHAT?

I was then shipped to Sheppard Field, Texas, where after three weeks I was called in for reassignment. The sergeant asked me what I wanted to do. I thought for something that would do two things: get me closer to home (New York City) and give me another crack at flying. I answered "aerial gunner." He said, "You got it. Only you need to train at one of the technical schools first, like radio, engineering or armorer." I replied, "What school is back east?" The sergeant said, "Radio" and I immediately replied, "Radio." Again, the sergeant said, "You got it." Thus, I wound up at Scott Field, Illinois, for radio mechanics.

On leave in July, I returned to the Bronx and on the 18th of July, 1943, married Helen Gentili, the girl I left behind when I enlisted. Then it was back to Scott Field to complete radio mechanics school. I graduated as a Radio Mechanic on October 14, 1943.

Now on to Chicago, Illinois for Morse Code stationed at Hotel Stevens, just off Lake Michigan, plush duty. Our duty consisted of being housed in a hotel room; up in the morning, breakfast in the hotel cafeteria and on to another nearby building for Morse Code training, and return to the hotel. Our room was cleaned and made up. At the end of a school day, supper at the cafeteria and enjoy the evening off, bed time; and next day, repeat the routine. How sweet it was! But it didn't last long, about a month and a half. I graduated December 30, 1944. Now I was a full-fledged radio operator.

I began gunnery training at Fort Myers, Florida, January 17, 1944, firing 50 caliber machine guns from turrets, learning how to lead targets, skeet-shooting and told how important we were, as with other crewmembers, depending on each other in combat. Our lives depended on how well we learned our lessons, what we learned was how to kill the pilot of enemy aircraft before they killed us, cruel and shocking, but war is hell. I earned my gunner's wings and my corporal rating on March 21, 1944.

GUNNER'S VOW

I wish to be a gunner

And you along with me,

For if we all were pilots,

where would the Air Force be?

It takes guts to be a gunner,

to sit in the tail

when the Messerschmitts are coming

and the slugs begin to wail.

The pilot's just a chauffeur,

it's his job to fly the plane.

But it's we who do the fighting

though we may not get the fame.

If we all must be gunners,

then let us make a bet

we'll be the best damned gunners

who have left this station yet.

(Author unknown)

Cpl. Joe Pace with Gunner's wings March 21, 1944

I Get to Fly Again!

Then it was on to Avon Park, Florida, in July, and on August 14, 1944 I was assigned to a heavy bomber, B-17 (the Flying Fortress), and met the nine other crew members for R.T.U. (Reserve Training Unit) training. Our crew consisted of:

2nd Lt. Gerald H. White – Pilot, single, conservative and serious, and an excellent pilot;

2nd Lt. Richard Peyton Woodson, III – Co-pilot, single, tall, polite, well-mannered, never said a cuss word and a great co-pilot;

2nd Lt. Carl Miller – Bombardier, married, blonde fellow on the quiet, serious side;

2nd Lt. Frank Voscinar – Navigator, married, oldest member of the crew and an excellent navigator;

Sgt. Jack Jayroe – Armorer/Gunner, single, authoritative, had pilot training, having washed out during cadet training;

Cpl. Carrol Johnson – Waist gunner, single, sort of a happy-go-lucky fellow, relaxed, easy to get along with;

Cpl. George D. Johnson – Tail gunner, single, very quiet,
more of a loner type guy;

Cpl. Victor Loesch – Engineer/gunner, single, very talkative
and pleasant to be with;

Cpl. Bob Fuller – Ball Turret gunner, single, youngest crew
member, shortest, of course, to fit in the ball, a very nice
person; and

myself, Cpl. Joseph D. Pace – Radio operator/gunner,
married, typical New Yorker, full of spunk and a bit of a
daredevil.

We called ourselves "The White's Crew." We flew practice
flights to familiarize ourselves with the B-17, how to fire our guns
(50 cal.), to communicate over the intercom. We wore what were
called "throat-mikes", strapped around our necks and tucked
under our chins. Our hands had to be free at all times to man the
machine guns.

We learned limits of the guns' firepower, the effectiveness of the
guns in fighting off the enemy coming too close to the formation.
We had to learn when to and when not to shoot during formation
flying, we had to be very careful not to shoot airplanes in our own
formation if they came into our line of fire. In practice flights over
the Everglades, our pilot, Lt. White, called on Jack Jayroe and me
to sit in the co-pilot's position and take control of the plane from
time to time. This was to determine if we would be able to control
the B-17 in the event of an emergency.

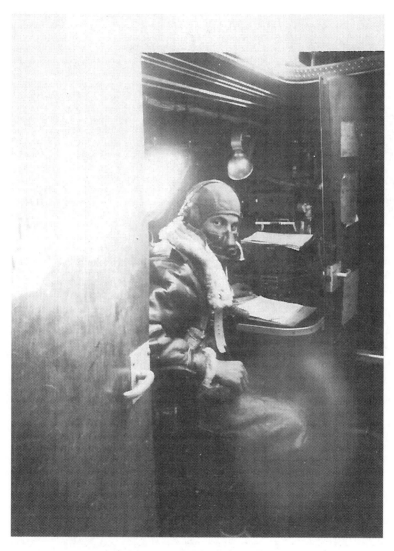

Pace at B-17 radio position in 1944

96th BOMB GROUP — 337th SQUADRON
AUGUST 1944

Standing L-R:

ROBERT FULLER	JACK JAYROE	VICTOR LOESCH	CARROLL JOHNSON	GEORGE JOHNSON	JOSEPH D. PACE
Ball Turret	Waist Gunner	Top Turret Gunner	Waist Gunner	Tail Gunner	Radio Operator
	(Armorer)	(Engineer)			

Kneeling L-R:

LT. FRANK VOSCINAR	LT. RICHARD PEYTON WOODSON, III	LT. GERALD H. WHITE	LT. CARL MILLER
Navigator	Co-Pilot	Pilot	Bombardier

Crew Picture

20

The "Flying Fortress"

The B-17 was known as the "Flying Fortress", nicknamed the "Fort", and weighed about 40,260 pounds according to the Boeing Aircraft Corporation, who built the B-17E, and could go 2,000 miles hauling a 4,000 pound bomb load cruising at 160 miles per hour. It is 73 feet, 9.1 inches long with a wingspan of 103 feet, 9.4 inches. It had four 1,200 horsepower engines made by Wright that would consume approximately 200 gallons of fuel an hour. Fuel capacity was 2,780 gallons. It was armed with eleven 50-caliber machine guns. Two are located in the nose of the plane manned by the bombardier. Two are in the top turret and manned by the engineer. Another gun is on the roof of the radio room and manned by the radio operator. Two more guns are in the waist on either side of the ship and manned by two waist gunners; and two machine guns are also in the ball turret under the belly of the ship manned by the ball turret gunner to defend from attacks below. The last two guns are in the tail of the ship manned by the tail gunner. Later the nose and the tail section was changed and fitted with 20mm cannons.

The Flying Fortresses typically fly in a formation called "the box". This mutually supportive formation often consists of a group of 28 to 30 planes staggered at slightly different altitudes. This gives the formation a menacing firepower because 300 or more machine guns interlock to make an attack suicidal. The last plane in the formation is known as "Tail-end Charlie." An actual bombing mission may be comprised of three, four, or more groups.

B-17 "Flying Fortress"

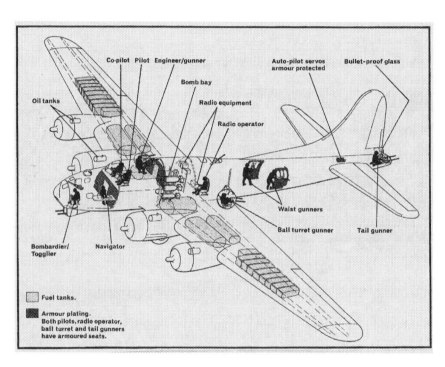

B-17 Crew and Equipment Locations

Practice Flights

We flew many practice formations flying over Central Florida and the Everglades. On a practice formation flight over Central Florida one day in August, 1944, when the flight was led by a new 1st Lt. Assistant Operations Officer, Jack Core, we flew into a thunder storm. It was late evening, there were strong winds and it was raining hard. Heading right into a thunderhead, we peeled away at the last minute. Lt. White went in for a landing at a field in Tampa. It was a difficult task and we skidded a long ways finally dropping off the end of the runway into the mud, nose down and finally up-righted. It was a harrowing experience to say the least. One plane broke apart and went down and another was so heavily damaged by hail that it had to be scrapped. One airman in the lost plane did not have a parachute, so he and the radio operator clung together and left the plane where it broke apart aft of the radio room. When the chute opened, the airman holding on lost his grip and was killed.

Another flight was for navigational practice cross-country to Will Rogers Air Field at Oklahoma City, Oklahoma. It was early evening when we landed and shut down the B-17. Lt. Gerald White mentioned that we wouldn't stay long – just refuel and return to our base at Avon Park, Florida. Most of the crew wasn't too happy with that and we all pleaded with the lieutenant to let us stay overnight. The lieutenant spoke with the crew chief and asked if he could find something to keep the B-17 grounded overnight and be ready to leave early in the morning. It worked. The delay was communicated to our home base. Lt. White gave us orders to be sure to be on time at 8:00 a.m. for our return, and if anyone was not on time the plane would leave without him. Victor Loesch and I buddied together and we had a great night. We each got a hotel room for the night and when I woke up the next morning it was 7:30; Victor was gone. "I'm going to be late! I'll miss the flight", I thought. I caught a taxi and told the driver to rush me to Will Rogers Airfield. Upon arrival, I looked out over the field and noticed our B-17 was slowly taxiing out. "Darn", I thought to myself, "the lieutenant really meant what he said." I jumped out of the cab, paid the driver and ran toward the plane. I saw Jack Jayroe at the waist door. He yelled out, "Run, Joe, run." He had his hand outstretched, got hold of my hand and yanked me into the plane. Whew, made it! Bob Fuller, our ball turret gunner, was occupying the radio station, he sighed, "Glad you're here; I didn't know what to do." We made the flight back to Avon Park in good shape.

Another practice flight was for target practice, how to lead an enemy fighter plane, and training for kills at 30,000 feet. You learn how to fire the 50-caliber machine gun at a cloth tube pulled behind a single trainer aircraft (I would not care to be that pilot) as a manner of teaching one how to lead an enemy aircraft. You fire in bursts with every fifth bullet being a red nose tracer bullet into a tube of cloth. This visibly allows you to adjust your aim should you be off target.

GOING OVER SEAS

Upon completion of our R.T.U. training, we were given a slick new B-17G and departed for England by way of the northern route. Ready to fly, we departed Avon Park, Florida, in the morning for Hunter Field at 10:00 a.m. on September 3, 1944. We were headed for Dow Field at Bangor Maine. Our pilot, Lt. White, had planned to do a fly-over of his folk's home on Grove Street, Valley Stream, New York. At 3:30 p.m. he did two 360-degree turns over it. But no one saw us – Lt. White was disappointed, as were all of us.

The weather was bad at Dow Field on September 4, 5 and 6, 1944, allowing no fly-outs. On the morning of September 7, 1944, we refueled and headed north for Goose Bay, Labrador. We flew over rough country for 500 miles. No towns or people all the way, closest town was Presque Isle. There was bad weather again on September 8 and 9, 1944. A story went about a falls in Labrador higher than Niagara Falls. On September 10, Bob Fuller, our ball turret gunner, was in the hospital for a cold. Bob Fuller was out of the hospital on September 11, 1944, and we were ready for take-off, but weather closed in on us and our flight was called off. We finally did leave Goose Bay on September 12, 1944, for Blue West 1, Greenland, leaving at 8:30 a.m. We stayed at Greenland base September 13 through 17 due to bad weather at Iceland.

At our stop in Greenland, Lt. Carl Miller, our bombardier,

took a walk around the area before supper and fell and broke his wrist. Most of the time we could see the shimmering of the bright Northern Lights at night. We were cleared to take off on September 18, 1944,. Sgt. Jack Jayroe used his charm with the nurses and managed to get our bombardier, Lt. Carl Miller, out of the hospital early that morning.

We headed to our next stop at Meeks Field, Iceland. What a place! The quarters were awful and darned cold. We were not welcome and were restricted to base. Iceland didn't like Americans, feeling we were intruders on their land. On September 19, 1944, we left Iceland for Valley, Wales. We left Iceland hungry; as our pilot said, "hungry as hell", no lunch. Glad to leave Iceland.

Our total flying time from Hunter Field to Valley, Wales, was 26 hours and 40 minutes. On September 20, 1944, we left Valley, Wales, for Stone, England.

BASE ASSIGNMENT & PROMOTIONS

When we arrived at Stone, England, we got orders assigning us to the 96th Bomb Group, 337th Squadron of the 8th Air Corps as Replacement Crew #95 (APO-16403-13J-95)

On September 25, 1944, we left the new B-17 and departing by truck, we arrived at Eccles Road, Snetterton Heath, our base of operation, near Norwich, England.

Our crew developed a very close relationship and we were ready to fly combat missions. Lt. Gerald White, our pilot, awarded the crew promotions; Tech Sgt. to Victor Loesch (engineer), Jack Jayroe (armorer) and me, Joseph D. Pace (radio operator). On September 28, 1944, the crew was cut down from 10 to 9. Lt. Gerald White had to release a crew member and Carroll Johnson, tail gunner, was the unlucky one and George Johnson became tail gunner with the waist gunner position eliminated.

It didn't take us long to become acquainted with the base mascot, Lady Moe, a donkey brought to the base by an enterprising crew returning from North Africa. (The full story on her acquisition can be found beginning on page 49 of "Snetterton Falcons.") We soon learned to appreciate this animal who had full run of the base. We found that among other things, she loved to eat cigarettes. There was a railroad running along the back side of the base and, unfortunately, this was one of Lady Moe's favorite haunts and during one of her ramblings there she was killed by a passing train.

Of course, she was given a "military funeral" and buried near the site of her demise.

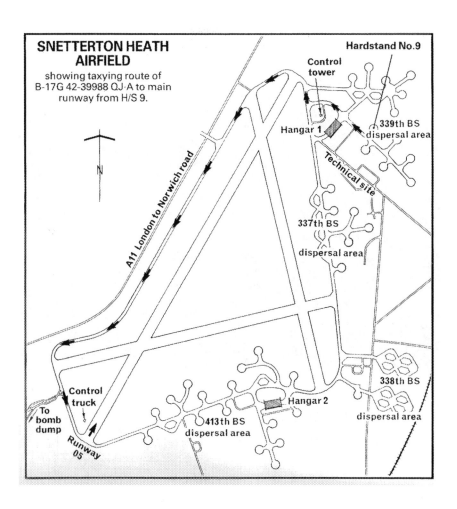

SNETTERTON HEATH AIRFIELD

showing taxying route of
B-17G 42-39988 QJ·A to main
runway from H/S 9.

N

Hardstand No.9

Control
tower

Control

Hangar 1

Technical site

339th BS
dispersal area

337th BS

dispersal area

A11 London to Norwich road

Control
truck

To
bomb
dump

Runway
05

413th BS
dispersal area

Hangar 2

338th BS

dispersal area

31

Crew Officers outside their hut with mascot "Stinky"

Lt. Carl Miller, Lt. Gerald White, Lt. Frank Voscinar and Lt. Richard Peyton Woodson III

Lt. Frank Voscinar feeding "Lady Moe" cigarettes

Brief History of the
96th Bomb Group

The 96th Bomb Group was activated on July 15, 1942. Crew training started at Boise, Idaho, on August 1, 1942 and other personnel began assembling at Walla Walla, Washington. The 96th started unit training on September 1 at Walla Walla. On October 1 the Group moved to Rapid City, South Dakota and the month of October was spent there before moving on to Pocatello, Idaho. Two months later they moved to Pyote, Texas. The 96th was the first unit on each of these bases.

After three months at Pyote they moved to Salina, Kansas, en route to the United Kingdom. The 96th deployed overseas with 30 aircraft, 15 crews and staff maintenance personnel that could be carried in the B-17s. The ground echelon remained at Pyote and arrived in England May 11, 1943.

The 96th was not supposed to fly any combat until the ground echelon arrived; however, the weather turned good after ten days so they started flying combat missions and flew six missions in the first seven days.

The 96th flew several of the better known missions during the war. Colonel Curtis E. Lemay rode with the 96th on the shuttle raid to North Africa, bombing Regensburg on the way over and Bordeaux on the way back on August 24, 1943. They led the first shuttle raid from England to Russia, bombing an oil refinery south

of Berlin en route. The 96th was in the lead on the S
mission of October 14, 1943, which is generally consi
the greatest air battle of the war with Germany with t
air forces sending up around 700 fighters against th
forces.

The 96th operated from Grafton Underwood for
then moved to Andrews Field at Great Saling, which v
American-built field in England. After spending on
Andrews they moved again to East Anglia, to Snette
where they remained until the summer of 1945 after th
they were deployed back to the United States.

96th BG statistics: Missions Flown – 321; Sorties Flo
Tons of Bombs dropped – 19,277; 190 Aircraft missin
50 Non-operational aircraft lost; 2nd highest loss in the
Command and the highest loss in the 3rd Division; 29
in combat.

COMBAT MISSIONS

⌐o ready for a combat mission, we would be awakened at 0300
hours, dress for flight, nylon heating suit under the heavy
⌐eepskin-lined leather suit, and go off for breakfast. This was
⌐e only meal for the day with flights of 8 to 10 hours' duration.
⌐en on to the briefing room. The Colonel would feed us the
⌐ormation, target on a large map, how many German fighter
⌐nes to expect, if any, how much "flak" to expect, and weather
⌐ormation and type of bombs. At the end of the briefing, the
⌐O. would ask for questions and, inevitably, someone would ask
⌐ny B-24s would be on the mission with our group. When a
⌐sitive answer was given, all the guys would yell out, "Hurray!"
⌐is was because German fighters would go after the B-24s first
⌐ they were an easier target, being larger and flying in a looser
⌐mation.

After leaving briefing, we picked up our parachutes and the
⌐ws would be trucked out to their respective aircraft, taking
⌐r assigned positions. When the take-off flare was fired into the
⌐ from the observer platform, the take-offs were at intervals of a
⌐nute apart and, invariably, at the end of the runway was a row of
⌐es to be cleared as we climbed to rendezvous with our squadron,
⌐th the 96th Bomb Group and then with other groups. At times,
⌐ B-17s and as many as 1,000 B-17s would be headed for the
⌐ssion. Flying to an altitude of 12,000 to 14,000 feet, we'd all go

on oxygen and plug into the electric system to heat the heating suit. At high altitudes, temperatures can get as low as -20, -40 and even -60 Fahrenheit; and that's COLD!

When approaching the combat zone, steel helmets and flak vests go on and all eyes are trained to all of the sky for enemy fighters. After surviving enemy fighters, it was now flak area. The pilot flies straight on into the I.P. (Initial Point) target area, without deviation. Upon reaching the target area, the pilot turns the aircraft over to the bombardier who has control until "Bombs Away". Then the pilot regains control of the aircraft. Now the return to home base is in reverse of the above except for the "Bombs Away." Should you survive all this, you have completed a mission. Should your crew survive 25 combat missions, you have the option to go for 25 more or be sent back to the States to sell war bonds and "tell all."

My combat tour in WWII in England lasted only 2-1/2 months, but there was always a feeling of apprehension that I could be killed, maimed or become a prisoner of war. And we had all heard tales of what happens to prisoners of war. Pushing such thoughts to the back of our minds, we proceeded with our duties and hoped for the best.

The planes in this "Wing" (96th Bomb Group) were distinguished by a large black square on the tail with the white square letter "C" on it. The group consisted of four squadrons sequentially numbered 337th, 338th and 339th, then jumps to 413th. The 413th came into play when the Army Air Corps combat Air Group consisted of 3 operational squadrons and one reconnaissance squadron. By 1942 the 413th squadron was eliminated as recon and joined with the 96th Bomb Group (H).

Our first mission was on October 9, 1944, to Mainz, Germany, east central Germany near Wiesbaden and Frankfurt on the Rhine River, near Luxembourg. We flew left wing of lead. Lt. Core flew left wing of high flight. Thirty-three of thirty-eight planes dispatched carried ten general purpose 500-pound bombs to target freight yards. Through 10/10ths cover PPF (Pathfinder radar for bombing through overcast) work well. NOE/A encountered light flak. No losses. We flew "Lovely Lady", #646A.

October 10, 1944, scheduled for a mission – scrubbed due to bad weather.

On October 10, 1944, a tragic incident occurred, a gunner cleaning his 50 caliber machine gun fired and shot Line Chief Howard Bresson's lower leg injuring it severely.

On October 11, 1944, scheduled for a mission – scrubbed due to bad weather.

On October 11, 1944, our plane, piloted by Lt. Gerald White, was flying right wing of the famous "Stingy" when three veteran Snetterton planes piled up in the skyways over Towcester in Northamptonshire. In this second training accident of the month the first B-17, a war weary plane #42-3510 piloted by Lt. Jack Core, nosed down to hit a plane, #43-37684, in the tail section. Just as plane #42-3510 was sheared in two, the famous "Stingy", #42-31052, compounded this unbelievable accident by hitting plane #43-37684 with its rudder. "Stingy" also broke in half. Lt. White took evasive action by peeling away immediately. Miraculously, the pilot of plane #43-3510, Lt. Jack Core, parachuted out safely while his plane and "Stingy" plummeted to earth in four sections. But his four crewmen were killed as were pilot Lt. P. Jorgenson and his "Stingy" crew of six. Although plane #43-37684 was severely damaged, it was eventually repaired. The loss of 12 fine airmen shocked the base.

(This account varies slightly from that published in "Snetterton Falcons, The 96th Bomb Group in World War II" by Robert E. Doherty and Geoffrey D. Ward inasmuch as information from R. Peyton Woodson, III, our co-pilot, is incorporated as he recalls the incident.)

Aircraft statistics October 1944:

October 11, 1944

A/C 42-3510

B-17 F-25 DL, 337th Squadron – AW-P

Mid-air training collision with 43-37684 and
42-31053, crashed at Wood End, Towcester,
Northants, England.

P. 2/Lt. Jack Core RTD

CP 2/Lt. Benjamin M. Bailey KLD

N 2/Lt. Richard M. McColl KLD

R T/Sgt. Kenneth F. LeBaron KLD

TT T/Sgt. Van H. Calvert KLD

P. N. Jorgenson plus his crew of six KLD,

One Airmen unknown

(Information taken from "Snetterton Falcons".)

Our second mission took place on October 12, 1944, and our
destination was Bremen in Northern Germany on the Weser River.
We flew the "All American Girl." Our bomb load was 6 general
purpose 1,000 lbs. The flak was moderate. There were abortions.
Ten dropouts. Only 26 B-17s of our group carried on to the target.
Lt. Earl Wynn, 338th, one of the dropouts, had to jettison his bombs
into an open field in Norfolk. Eleven of the bombs exploded. No
damage was reported and, for sure, the UXB (unexploded bomb)
boys went after the 12th bomb.

For a change, it was good weather over the target, a tank factory,
and bombardiers were pleased with their work. Flak damaged
some aircraft one of which was Lt. Marty Clayman's "Pilgrim's
Progress" which had to land at Seething, a B-24 base. But cripples
couldn't be choosy. Clayman's bombardier, Lt. Nash, was slightly
wounded. Sgt. H.A. Weaver was wounded in the face aboard Lt.
Perlis' 338th Fort.

Our third mission took place on October 14, 1944; destination,
Cologne in East-Central Germany near Belgium on the Rhine River,

a frequent target because of harboring the busiest rail junction on the Franco-German border. Orders were not to destroy the famous cathedral of Cologne. Cologne kept toughing out the war. The most horrific raid had been the night of 28-29 June, 1943, when Bomber Command sent 608 RAF heavies to destroy over 6,000 buildings. Over 400 people had been killed back then and over the following weeks, more than 230,000 were made homeless.

That day was the first of a triple-hit on Cologne with American forces flying during the day and the British at night. We flew the "All American Girl", 981-K, and carried four IP (Initial Point) and fourteen 250 lb. general purpose bombs. Except for a brief mix-up when each group became oblivious to the other during the bomb run, this raid was rather routine. Early on, Captain Charles Shaw, 339th, had to abort, but he landed safely in Brussels.

Our 4th mission out was October 15, 1944. Again, the destination was Cologne, Germany. Aborts were suddenly plaguing the group. Only 28 of the 35 planes dispatched made it to Kalk Nord Marshalling yards. Bombs were slightly off the MPI (Main Point of Impact desired) due to contrails. Only the southern end of the yards was hit. From there, the bombs trailed into the adjacent village of Vingst. Flak was moderate, but it was our first real flak damage hit. No losses. We flew the "All American Girl" and carried 4 IP and sixteen 250-pound general-purpose bombs, returning with two flak holes.

We flew the "Reluctant Dragon" on our 5th mission on October 17, 1944. Cologne, Germany was the target. We carried two IP and thirty-four 100-pound general-purpose bombs. The Cologne raids took place over five days and we were on three of those.

Bad weather had provided a day of rest before the third straight raid on the cathedral city. Once more, the "abort gremlins" sent five planes homeward prematurely. Because of the haze over the Kifeller yards, the thirty-one planes followed PFF (Pathfinder radar for bombing through overcast) procedure and cameras recorded a good strike. Some returning crews watched a P-51 down a German defender. The German plane was hit at 20,000 feet and disintegrated.

During that day's debriefing, everyone begged the "powers that be" to stop mixing up crews. When bombardiers and Mickey Operators ((radar operators) flew together on a regular basis, they argued, the results were good. Post-strike photos proved they were right.

On October 25, 1944, Hamburg, Germany, was our sixth mission. Lt. Carl Miller, bombardier, having recovered from a broken wrist back on September 17th, flew with us for the first time. The target was in Northern Germany on the Elbe River. We carried twenty 250-pound general-purpose bombs. Following another PFF operation, two large columns of smoke convinced crews that they had plastered Hamburg's oil refineries. The knowledge was a confidence builder because only radar images and gut feelings had sustained them recently. All returned safely although there were three with flak damage. Our plane, #621(O), lost its #2 engine, but we feathered the prop and stayed to return with the squadron. Flak was heavy but not near us.

Merseburg, Germany was our seventh mission. It was October 30, 1944 and we carried sixteen general-purpose 300-pound bombs. We flew lead low flight, #740-G. The location of the target was in East-Central Germany, near Leipzig. On this day, the 3rd Air Division demanded that the 96th bomb group put up more bombers than we had during the whole month. A "Biggie" was scheduled. But over Holland, a messy frontal system forced 400 bombers to turn back. Only weather ever caused the 8th Air Corps to turn back.

The bombs on this mission were all returned to base except for the 339th Squadron plane piloted by Lt. Ricke. He was loaded with the big bombs with the long nose and was ordered to jettison them in the North Sea. Although recalled and brought back and landing with a full load of bombs, we were credited for this mission.

B-17 Group Flying on a Mission

B-17 Encountering German Flak

A Little R&R Time

Our crew was awarded a 72-hour pass for R&R on November 2, 1944 and we all boarded the LNER (London Northeastern Railroad) train, with tracks that passed by the rear of our base, at the little Eccles Road Station near Snetterton Heath for London. Arriving in London, we split into separate groups and Tech. Sgt. Victor Loesch, our top turret gunner and engineer, and I paired off. We had a great time visiting the sights of London, Picadilly Square, London Bridge, the Westminster Abbey, Buckingham Palace, and the House of Parliament, et cetera.

Vic and I rented a hotel room for the night and the following morning we showered and readied for breakfast. Walking down the street in London, a young new lieutenant (90-day wonder) approached us with a sergeant. I said to Vic we better salute this young new lieutenant. We did and the lieutenant returned the salute. No sooner had he passed us by than he turned back, stopped and ordered us to show our dog-tags. Well, Vic showed his from around his neck. Oh, no, I knew I was in trouble remembering that before I showered I had placed my dog-tags in my pants pocket. I tried to explain but the lieutenant chewed me out for not wearing them around my neck. He commenced asking me if a German buzz-bomb exploded in my vicinity and I was killed, how would I be identified. I responded, "Sir, if a buzz bomb exploded here no one would be able to identify me anyway." Wrong answer! The expression on his face let me know he didn't like my answer so I said, "I guess you will be reporting me to my C.O." However, he said he'd let it ride this time and said, "Make sure your dog-tags are around your neck at all times." I thanked the lieutenant and we saluted.

Eccles Road Train Station

WHAT? KP?

Returning to base on November 4, I was shocked to learn I was ordered to pull KP for a day. That lieutenant hadn't kept his word. But I don't recall working very hard. At the end of my day I decided to ask the culinary sergeant for food for the crew, bread, butter and apples. By now the sergeant was getting annoyed with me, but while in the refrigerator getting the apples, I noticed fully plucked chickens, so I secreted two of them under my flight jacket. When I was going to ask for more food, he angrily said, "Get the Hell out of here."

Returning to my Nissen hut, which housed two combat crews, I shouted out "food!" There was an old oil drum in which wood was burning to heat the hut. We got an open gallon can, placed the butter in it and cooked the chickens and enjoyed a "feast".

Back to Business

Joining 31 other aircraft, we carried 6 general purpose 1,000 pound bombs on our eighth mission on November 5, 1944. Our target was the Ludwigshaven marshalling yards in southeastern Germany on the Rhine River near Mannheim. This winter day developed into slanting rain and bitter, windy chill. Inclement weather in England did not prevent the group from bombing Germany. A small opening in the clouds presented bombardiers opportunity to use visual sightings. Although the MPI (main point of impact desired) was missed, bombs did fall within the designated target area. Lt. Fred Whitney, 413th Squadron, could not keep pace with the group due to cylinder temperature problems. Even so, he fell in with the 447th Squadron and did his job.

Over the target area, unidentified fighters were spotted, called-out and fired upon by eager gunners. Immediately, they identified themselves as P-51 Mustangs. Coming at our formation straight on was not the thing to do. Careless fighter pilots who forgot to show a good silhouette to bomber formations ran the risk of being subjected to friendly fire.

While we were over the target area, we were plagued by two engine failures requiring us to leave formation and head alone for home base. An intensive frontal system had developed over Snetterton-Heath so we were diverted to Feresfield Air Base.

Flying low over the English Channel, we received a challenge over the radio from a British Navy ship inquiring as to whether we were friend or foe. We were returning home alone due to an engine problem and it was past 5 p.m., at which time our identification code changed, and I had failed to obtain the code change prior to leaving on the mission. Realizing the code I did have would be unacceptable, I called up to the pilot and asked what I should do. He replied, "send it." I did and the British commenced firing at us. Fortunately, we weren't hit.

But now we were not sure of finding Feresfield and our pilot spotted an open area on the coastline that looked like a base. He said, "We're going in. Prepare for landing." We landed on a dirt runway, and shortly thereafter our engines stopped. I think we ran out of fuel. Suddenly, we heard the roar of trucks and people yelling at us to get out and get into the trucks. We had to leave all our gear behind with the B-17 and were immediately taken by truck to our home base.

We later learned that Feresfield was a secret training base for volunteer pilots to take off in remote controlled war-weary B-17s that were not fit to fly combat missions. The war weary bombers would be crammed with TNT and other types of high explosives and be flown toward specific German targets such as V-1 and V-2 rockets installations, radar stations or 88mm anti-aircraft cannon locations. The pilots would then bail out while still in friendly territory letting the plane continue on remote control hoping they would hit the targeted areas and cause massive destruction.

Paratroopers normally bail out of the wide door of the aircraft at about 100 mph. However, in this project, called the Aphrodite project, the volunteer pilots had to bail out through the small navigator's hatch, known as the nose hatch, while the plane was speeding at 170-200 mph. No easy task.

The 32 aircraft of our mission returned safely, but 17 had minor flak damage and five had major damage. Flak was heavy and dense. The intense frontal system over Snetterton-Heath had forced five A/C to land eastward at Beccles Leiston and Woodbridge.

Our 9th mission was November 6, 1944, to Duisburg, Germany. Once more the new MICRO H (electronic assistance on the bomb run, using beacon) Pathfinder technique helped the Eighth sustain a successful November campaign against the enemy's fuel supply. The primary target was the Teerverwertung Benzol Plant in East-Central Germany near Dusseldorf. German flak was expected to be heavy. Our plane was one of the 96th's C Group, which consisted of six A/C plus one PFF (Pathfinder radar for bombing through overcast). We made a chaff run over the target before the main force carrying only chaff, no guns, no ammo and no bombs. The mission was to drop the chaff over the target to foil the German radar 10 minutes ahead of the main bombing formation. We all returned to base safely. The strategy worked. Most flak was inaccurate. Unfortunately, one stray flak fragment entered T/Sgt. Martin Organtini's top turret on Lt. Al Hillier's 337th Squadron plane and killed the engineer/gunner. Out of the 30 effective A/C this day, only four returned with minor damage.

Our tenth mission was November 10, 1944, and the Luftwaffe base at Erbenheim near Wiesbaden, Germany, was our target. We carried 36 general purpose 100-pound bombs. Bombs were dropped on German ground support to support General Patton advances. Not much flak but very accurate. We saw a 338th A/C go down and we returned with two flak holes.

Victor Loesch, our top turret gunner/engineer, did not fly with us on this mission as he was in the hospital recovering from the burned hand he received on a practice mission. In that practice mission a wire in the bomb bay had an electrical wire shorted and Victor tugged at it to break the connection preventing further catastrophe. Unfortunately, his hand was seriously burned. So we had a replacement flying in Victor's position. Lt. White later expressed regret at not being able to submit a commendation or request a medal of some sort to be awarded to Victor Loesch for his brave action since it did not occur during a combat mission.

After the return of every mission sergeants would be standing at the front door to the de-briefing room and pour a double shot of bourbon. This was to relax us so we'd spill our guts out and tell what happened, how accurate the flak was, if any, any B-17s went down and any airmen parachuted out and over what area, what type of German fighters, et cetera. George Johnson of our crew did not drink alcohol so his double bourbon went to one of the rest of the crew on an alternating basis allowing one of us to receive a double double shot.

MY 11ᵀᴴ & FINAL WWII MISSION

It was November 21, 1944, and I had completed ten missions with my regular crew. They were out without me for a weather report and needed a radio operator meteorologist, which I was not. So I was sleeping in at 3 a.m. when a sergeant came calling my name. Upon awakening, I was told I had been assigned to fly replacement radio operator with a crew piloted by Lt. Jack Core of the 337th. Bearing in mind the incident in a training mission at Avon Park, Florida, and the mid-air training incident of October 11, 1944, where three veteran Snetterton B17s piled up, and in which Lt. Core parachuted to safety leaving his crew to die, I was reticent to be a part of his crew. But I had no choice. I was told, "Go or face court martial." Adding to my concerns was the fact that the other eight crewmembers were on their first mission.

This then became my eleventh mission and we were to bomb oil installations at Mersburg, Germany. After breakfast and briefing, we with our gear and chest parachutes were trucked to our assigned 'fort. As usual, it was very early in the morning, about 4 a.m. and still dark with many more B-17s lined up in single file readying for take off, spaced at one minute intervals, waiting for the green flare, and to rally into proper formation before heading for the target. It was a cold, clear day.

We were up and flying, rallying for our respective positions. While sitting in position at the radio desk with only a dim light, taking Morse Code, I caught a glimpse of something off the corner of my left eye. I quickly turned to the small window and there shone a brilliant light. Suddenly, the face of Jesus Christ appeared brilliantly and came closer and closer. Then, just as it had appeared, it began to slowly disappear until it was gone. I hadn't considered myself a particularly religious person, even though I was a Roman Catholic, but this was quite unsettling and I had this terribly eerie feeling that something was going to happen on that mission. It's a vision I will never forget as long as I live. Every time I talk about this I get a tingling sensation throughout my body. In later years in telling about this incident with our pastor at St. Luke's Lutheran Church in La Mesa, California, I came to realize that this was God's way of showing me that, yes, something was going to happen, but Jesus would be there to see me through this sea of evil and bring me safely home.

We were at 20,000 feet between Hanover and the IP when we received a recall due to a severe frontal system. The 1AD (First Air Division) had already gone in under the clouds and now they were coming out – groups were piling up behind, crossing each other in all directions trying to avoid collisions. One of the B17s in the formation was turned over by "prop-wash" from another B17 crossing over it. It spun out of formation. After several spins, it attempted to pull out, but broke in half at the radio room. The B-17 exploded in mid air. There were no survivors.

Foiled by the weather, the unbearable prop wash and the fatal air traffic conditions, the group turned back and selected the secondary target, Osnabruck's marshalling yards.

The 337th Squadron plane 42-97981, piloted by Lt. Jack Core, in which I was flying as replacement radio operator, had left the formation earlier from the main group due to engine failure, but had bombed a target of opportunity at Koblenz, Germany, the marshalling yard, which was confirmed by the 122 Wing of the RAF, Royal Air Force. After the Koblenz bombing, the pilot deemed that return to England was impossible. We were losing altitude and word came over the intercom from Lt. Core to jettison all unnecessary equipment to lighten the plane. Guns, ammo, any loose armor plates, anything that was loose was ripped up, torn and thrown away. As radio operator, assuming we were now in friendly air space, I was constantly signaling "Mayday" so others might fix our position. Lt. Core headed the plane for the English Channel for possible ditching.

Finally, Lt. Core, issued the frightening order across the intercom, "Pilot to crew: Bail out." However, the emergency bail out bell was never activated. Receiving the bail-out order, I yelled to the tail gunner and two waist gunners, who were busy jettisoning equipment, to grab their chutes and bail out.

The tail gunner, two waist crew members and I headed for the waist door. I pulled the emergency door release handle but the door did not fly off as it was supposed to do. So we all headed for the bomb bay and found the bomb bay doors to be opened only six inches. Recalling what I had heard from other airmen that jumping on the doors with a weight of 150 pounds or more would extend the opening, even though I weighed no more than 130 pounds, I jumped on it thinking I might get through and the rest could follow. No such luck; the door would not give way. The only other exit I could think of was the nose hatch. One airman, the tail gunner, said he was going to the tail gunner section to bail out. I said, "Good luck." Another airman got by the top turret and bailed out of the nose hatch. Following him, I got snagged in the top turret area. The airman behind me saw the situation and freed me so I could finally get to the nose hatch. Looking about, I was shocked when I noticed that all members of the crew up front, the pilot, all of the officers, engineer, armorer, and ball turret gunner, had already bailed out. We were incredibly low.

Estimating my altitude to be somewhat less than 300 feet, I was afraid I wouldn't survive a free fall jump, but I didn't like the idea of going down with the plane and crashing either. So I decided to "go for it". As I was hanging outside the nose hatch with the earth appearing to be closing in on me, I pondered what to do. Should I let go and pull my parachute ripcord as I fall away from the plane or pull it immediately as I break away? Thinking if I do and the chute deploys fast, it may hit the plane's tail section and I'm a goner, I decided to take a chance on pulling the ripcord as soon as I let go of the nose hatch. As I pulled the ripcord, I thought to myself,

"I'm dead." The ground was coming up fast and I kept falling and falling. The chute popped open just as my left foot touched the ground, saving my life.

RESCUE

It was about 5:30 p.m. and the sky was beginning to darken. Lying on the ground stunned and feeling no pain, I looked over towards my left and noticed my leg and ankle were in an awkward position. It must be broken. Unable to get up, I managed to gather my chute in and place it under my head. After awhile I saw figures of people at a distance and didn't know if they were German soldiers or civilians. Here I am with no way to protect myself, no .45 automatic weapon. The C.O. had ordered all .45 weapons turned in. His reasoning being that without a weapon you would have a better chance of being interned alive. I was concerned that if they were civilians I might be pitch forked to death. Stories were floating about of such acts by civilians. The group was getting closer when I heard three explosions and then the group disappeared. Later I again saw the group approaching very slowly. As they got nearer I recognized the British uniform and felt great relief; now I knew I would not be a POW. First to approach was a British Sergeant and he asked, "Were there any others in the aircraft after you jumped?" I replied, "Yes, one." He responded that he did not see anyone parachute out after me and he hadn't expected to find me alive as he estimated I had left the plane at about 150 feet and he hardly knew anyone would survive a jump under 300 feet free-fall. He also said the one airman who parachuted out before me was killed on impact. They found him with his hand still on the ripcord handle and surmised he froze when he jumped. The airman behind me, obviously, never left the plane, going down with the plane to his death. The two killed on this mission were waist gunners S/Sgt. Joseph E. Bradshaw and S/Sgt. Lowell E. Warmich.

Leaning over me, the British sergeant asked if I had any morphine. As I said, "Yes", he removed it from my parachute harness strap, broke the glass vial and injected the morphine into my left arm. Next he lit a British cigarette and was about to place it in my mouth as I vehemently protested, "I don't smoke." He responded, "Shut up, Bloke", and stuck it between my lips. I questioned him about the three explosions and he informed me that I was in a German mine field, one of their men had stepped on a mine and almost got his leg blown off. They got him back to the hospital, then returned for me. He said the Germans almost always wired the land mines in a series of three. I had landed just inside the border of Holland near a town called Eindhoven. The British had just chased the Germans out that week and they had not gotten all the mine fields cleared. I was fortunate to have fallen in friendly territory.

Using a broken barn door as a makeshift stretcher, they covered me with old blankets and gingerly carried me off. I was taken to a Royal Air Force hospital where the doctor told me I had a "Potts" fracture and that he would set it for me and place a cast around it. The cast turned out to cover all the way up to my knee.

Unfortunately, this incident was reported in the 1989 issue of "Snetterton Falcons" at page 504 as follows: "The 337th's 42-97981 piloted by Lt. Jack Core had left formation earlier due to the bad weather but had bombed a target of opportunity at Koblenz which was confirmed by 122 Wing of the Royal Air Force. But engine trouble made return to England impossible.

The plane was put on AFCE while the crew bailed out over friendly territory near Ulden, Holland. All were OK and even the plane was later salvaged by the 5th Air Division."

Well, I'm here to tell you I was on that plane and was fortunate to have lived through it and that report just isn't quite the way it really happened. As to any salvage of the plane, I've been told in recent years by Robert E. Doherty, author, writer, 96th Bomb Group editor, publisher and historian 8th Air Force Historical Society, regarding the report in the Snetterton Falcon publications that "salvage" did not necessarily mean the restoration of a plane. The term was also used to mean that "treasures" such as engines, guns, et cetera, were salvaged from the wreckage. Be that as it may, I distinctly heard an explosion on impact after going over trees. And the British sergeant who saw the incident said they couldn't get near the B17 due to the intense fire and heat, and that .50 caliber bullets were popping about at the front of the plane.

At the Royal Air Force Hospital, having a rating of Tech/Sgt., I was considered an officer by British standards and placed in a room with a wounded Royal Air Force fighter pilot. During my three days in the RAF hospital, the young volunteer nurses would take turns entering the room pretending to dust just to see an American. The English food didn't set well with my American tastes so I gave most of it to the pilot in my room. I also gave him all of my chocolates and cigarettes received from the British Red Cross. The chocolates were for his five-year-old daughter that he hadn't seen in his five years of combat. He was to be released to go home just before Christmas of 1944.

Scabies – What's That?

After three days in the RAF hospital I was shipped out by flight in a C-47 (the Air Corps military workhorse) to a U.S. general hospital in Oxford near London, England for continued treatment. About a week later my whole body began itching. It got so bad I drew blood from scratching so hard. It was discovered that I had a very infectious and contagious skin disease called "Scabies", and I was immediately isolated. I questioned how I got scabies and was told it could be from dirty clothing, blankets, et cetera. I probably got it from those old blankets the British used to cover me on that makeshift stretcher.

Following three or more days of treatment I was released from isolation and returned to a regular ward where I was awarded the Purple Heart for injury sustained in combat.

Pain Relief!

There were lots of wounded infantrymen in the U.S. General Hospital. One night near mid-night, I heard an infantryman near my bed moaning and sobbing. Soon after the nurse appeared and questioned the wounded soldier. He responded, "I'm hurting real bad." He was told to be quiet and she would be back with something to quell his pain. When she returned I noticed she had a shot glass with bourbon. After the drink he quieted down and went to sleep. Seeing this I thought I'd give it a try. Well, sure enough, I got a shot of bourbon for my "pain." I have to say that the nurses were the greatest, they really took good care of us. They were fast-learners too. Those of us who were bed-ridden found a unique way to communicate our needs when the urge to urinate occurred. We'd yell out "Need a P-51." They soon learned what the air crewmen meant by a P-51 and brought us a urinal.

Well, Hello, Crewmembers!

On November 25, 1944 while I was at the U.S. General Hospital at Oxford, England, our pilot, Lt. Gerald White, requisitioned a "war weary" B-17 (an aircraft that can fly but is no longer combat worthy) and flew some of my crew members up for a visit. Was I surprised to see them. There was the Pilot Lt. Gerald White, with Co-pilot Lt. R. Peyton Woodson III, Navigator Lt. Frank Voscinar, and Engineer Tech. Sgt. Victor Loesch. Of course, they also had a replacement radio operator. They even brought "Stinkie" the dog, our mascot. At this time, I related to Lt. White what happened going down on the eleventh mission with Lt. Jack Core.

Still using crutches, I was able to pose for some pictures taken by one of the crew. It was great seeing them. We never got together again as a group until many years later at Eighth Air Force reunions. We did, however, manage to stay in touch by mail.

While still in the hospital I received word of the birth of my son Raymond born February 7, 1945.

Surprise Crew Visit to U.S. General Hospital at Oxford, England, near London January 17, 1945.

Pictured back row: Lt. Gerald White, Lt. R. Peyton Woodson, III, Tech. Sgt. Pace, Sgt. George Johnson; Front row: unknown radio operator and Lt. Frank Voscinar

Wounded Tech. Sgt. Joe Pace at Oxford Hospital

Purple Heart and Air Medal

HOME SWEET HOME

Every month the medical doctor would come in and discuss the injury. Asked if they healed me soon would I like to return to my original outfit or be reassigned, I said I preferred returning to my regular crew. However, three months later I was still not healing fast enough and was told I'd be returning to the States for continued treatment. That meant home. I was so elated that the war was over for me for the time being.

My return to the United States was on the HMS Queen Elizabeth, which had been converted into a hospital ship. Thousands of wounded servicemen were aboard the ship. Released from the hospital, I was placed in a U.S. hospital vehicle and caravan and headed for Port of South Hampton, England. On the way the caravan was stopped and I heard my name being shouted out, "Tech. Sgt. Joseph D. Pace", several times. I thought, "Oh, no, am I going to be pulled out and returned to the hospital?" Then the young (weren't we all?) Second Lieutenant and his sergeant opened the door to the ambulance and again asked for Tech. Sgt. Joseph D. Pace. I answered, "Yes, Sir". He said, "All I need from you is the overpayment." I replied, "Lieutenant, you can have all of my money; I'm going home." The lieutenant replied, "Oh no, just the overpayment." That was completed and we were on our way again.

Three days out to sea we had a German submarine alert. The

ship made a complete stop in the dead of night. Later the captain announced over the intercom that the alert was over and we were again underway, he advised us not to worry as it would take three direct hits of the German submarine torpedoes to sink the ship.

Arriving in New York Harbor on the fifth day, there were all kinds of crafts alongside escorting us into the harbor: fireboats, tugs, et cetera, tooting, blasting their foghorns and water cannons shooting water up into the air. Quite a sight! The ultimate was seeing that "Grand Lady", the Statue of Liberty. Very emotional.

Finally docking at Staten Island, the ship captain announced for all of us to dress in full uniform as much as possible. German POWs assisted us off the ship and into a U.S. general hospital. We were surprised seeing MPs checking us for weapons, any ammo, bayonets and any other contraband; all were confiscated. Naturally, I lost my .45 caliber hand gun and ammo clips that I had acquired.

A Nice Surprise!

After getting settled in the hospital, I received a visit from Grace White, Lt. Gerald White's mother. Before she located me, she entered the wardroom from the information she had been given and asked for Joseph Pace. She received an answer from another individual who was also Joseph Pace. They quickly realized he was not the one she was seeking and he asked, "Are you looking for my cousin?" She eventually found me and through her I learned my cousin was here also. He had been wounded across the stomach by German machine gun bullets. We had a nice visit and, of course, she asked me about her son. I must add that Lt. White's mother was a very lovely lady with whom we maintained contact until her death quite a number of years later.

Rest & Recovery

A month later I was shipped to Pawling in upstate New York to an Air Corps recuperating hospital. The facility was the property of New York's governor, Thomas E. Dewey, on loan to the U.S. Air Corps for the sole purpose for Air Corps servicemen to recover mentally and physically and treatment for eventual return to active duty or discharge from the service.

While recuperating we were allowed to do just about anything we pleased. Signs on the grass read, "Please walk on the grass." Hobbies of all kinds, horseback riding, golfing, you name it. Pets were even available. I received a pedigree German Shepherd puppy with papers. The food was excellent and plentiful. The mess hall remained open all day so we could eat anytime.

When Germany surrendered May 8, 1945, (VE Day) I had enough service points to qualify for a discharge, but I was retained because we were still at war with Japan and my M.O. as a radio operator and gunner was essential.

DISCHARGE AT LAST

Japan surrendered on September 2, 1945 and I finally received my honorable discharge on October 15, 1945. I still needed the aid of my GI cane for walking. As a matter of fact, I still have it even today. The medals I received for my military service were the Purple Heart for injuries received, Air Medal for flying combat, European Theater of Operation medal, the Efficiency, Honor, Fidelity (Good Conduct) medal, the American Campaign medal and the Victory World War II medal.

Although my mother was in poor health for many years, she lived to see all three of her sons return home from the war before her death January 25, 1947.

The following is an excerpt from the "Snetterton Falcons" by Roger A. Freeman of Dedham, England, August 1989:

"In the 8th Air Force the largest and most famous band of American Sky Warriors --- (the 96th Bomb Group) had the highest casualties and definitely the loss of more aircrafts to enemy action than any other of the 40-odd bomb groups in the 8th Air Force."

All of our original crew returned home at the end of World War II, including the replacement radio operator, Tech. Sgt. Otis Haslop.

THE WAR WAS OVER BUT - -

I was out walking in full uniform with my German Shepherd dog in Brooklyn, New York, one day, the same one I acquired during my hospital stay at Pawling, New York. A woman was looking out her window on the second story and called out, "Soldier, Soldier, what kind of dog you got?" I replied, "A German Shepherd." Immediately, she spat down towards the dog. I said, "Lady, it's just a dog." She said, "German!" Obviously, she was very prejudiced.

Passing On

Our crew was fortunate that we never had any serious incidents as we flew combat missions and/or practice missions with our own crew. Our injuries were sustained while flying replacement with other crews giving credence to our belief that ours was the best crew in the outfit. And we all came home alive.

Since our return home, we have lost some members of the crew; Cpl. Carroll Johnson (waist gunner), Lt. Carl R. Miller (bombardier), Tech/Sgt. Victor E. Loesch (engineer/top turret gunner), Frank Voscinar (navigator), and Cpl. Bob Fuller (ball turret gunner). Although they have passed on, they are not forgotten. May they rest in peace. Five of our original crew remain and are currently in our 80s.

At this time, World War II vets are passing away at the rate of 2,000 per day. Hard to believe, but true. This information was passed on to Ann Landers just prior to Memorial Day, 2001, by a fellow named Mike in Chantilly, Virginia. He had been given a poem by one of his Army buddies and asked Ann Landers to print it in the newspaper. She didn't let him down. She printed the poem titled "Just a Common Soldier." It spoke of a balding old fellow with a paunch who sat round the Legion telling stories about a war he and his buddies had fought. They agreed that they were heroes as they listened because the Legion buddies all knew what he was talking about. It goes on to say that one day they'd hear his stories no longer because "Old Bill has passed away" making the world a little poorer because a soldier's part in time of conflict is to clean up troubles that others often start. At the end it states we should give him homage or "Perhaps a simple notice in a paper that would say, 'Our country is in mourning 'cause a soldier passed away."

LIFE AFTER THE WAR

L ife goes on and I finally found employment in New York City working for Beltone for awhile, but did not care for the position. So I went through an employment agency and found a position with a newly developing industry working with plastics. I was learning the operations of the machinery when my mother became quite ill and I took a leave of absence. Upon my return I was asked to work as traffic manager of their shipping operation.

During this time my wife's brother was urging us to move to Chillicothe, Ohio, and live in the country, get out of the city. She took our son and went for a visit with her brother and her sister, who were living there. When she returned, she had left the baby with her sister and was intent on moving to Ohio. So we moved to Chillicothe.

I was unemployed and searched for a job eventually working for Albertson's Supermarket as a stock clerk. Shortly thereafter my brother-in-laws learned that the Federal Reformatory in Chillicothe had openings for correctional officers and they enticed me to go along and apply with them. I wasn't particularly enthusiastic about the idea and was surprised when I was hired. This began my career in the Federal Prison System. During our stay in Chillicothe, our second son, Ronald Paul, was born on October 4, 1948.

In November, 1951, I was asked to transfer to Florence, Arizona, to participate in reactivation of an old WWII POW camp about four miles out of town. By Thanksgiving, I was in Florence while my wife was finishing up the sale of our home in Chillicothe and packing up the two boys to fly to Phoenix to join me. It was at this station that I was promoted to Senior Correctional Officer. It was also in Florence that we began experiencing marital difficulties and separated in June of 1955. We were divorced on September 14, 1955.

Now, I was a bachelor again and moved into bachelor officers' quarters at the Florence Federal Prison. Later another bachelor and I shared housing on the prison grounds.

SINGLE BUT NOT FOR LONG

Word came that a young blonde had arrived in Florence. All the eligible bachelors were anxious to date this newcomer to the community and I made up my mind that I was going to somehow make her acquaintance. I learned that her name was Thelma Podell and she was working at the office of the County Attorney. As fate had it, my son Raymond was admired by the 12-year-old daughter of the family with whom Thelma was residing. It was May of 1956 and the 12-year-old girl hosted a party that my son Raymond attended. Thelma helped make the party a success and the girl's mother, Mrs. Hurley, insisted on taking Thelma out for a Coke. Now, you have to understand that Florence, Arizona, was a very small town with a population of about 2,000 and the only place one could buy a Coke after 9 p.m. was at a bar. Thus, she and Thelma came into the Oak Tavern and Thelma ordered a 7-Up. I happened to be nursing a beer at the end of the bar. Well, I wasn't going to let this opportunity pass, so I sidled on down toward them and spoke to Mrs. Hurley, who promptly introduced me to Thelma. I managed to stay with her for the rest of the evening during which we played snooker and she beat me and a number of others all the while proclaiming she'd never played the game before. No matter, I decided this was "it," this was the girl I was going to marry! Which I did on July 18, 1956.

Thelma and I moved to Long Beach, California, in August

of 1956 where I had accepted a transfer to the Terminal Island Federal Correctional Institution. In 1957 we purchased a home in Westminster, California. Our daughter, Carmela Jean, was born on June 4, 1959.

Having accepted a transfer to the Federal Correctional Institution located at Lompoc, California, we moved up there in January of 1960. Our son, Jonathan Joseph, was born on October 25, 1961. During my tenure at the Lompoc Federal Correctional Institution I was promoted to Senior Officer Specialist.

I retired from the Federal Prison Service November 1, 1970, and we continued to live in Lompoc until June of 1981. During this time I obtained my real estate license and worked selling residential real estate. I also took additional courses and obtained my real estate broker's license and, later, my designation as GRI (Graduate of Realtor's Institute). At my urging, Thelma studied for and obtained her real estate license in 1978. We worked together in the same office, during which Thelma continued her real estate education and obtained her broker's license also.

Following our move to La Mesa, California, in June of 1981, we continued working together at the San Carlos office of Coldwell Banker. Thelma also studied for and obtained her GRI designation after our move to La Mesa. Eventually we both retired from the real estate field and took life a bit easier.

Grandparents

Our daughter, Carmela, was married to James M. Ward on August 7, 1982, and on May 22, 1991, they presented us with our first grandchild, Christopher James Ward. We found we really enjoyed being grandparents and were quite pleased when Pamela Jean Ward appeared on the scene on September 24, 1996. They live very near and we get to enjoy them on an almost daily basis.

WE VISIT GERMANY

On July 25, 1997, my wife Thelma and I left on a tour of Germany that took us on a ground tour of several of the cities bombed by our crew as well as the one of my last mission over Koblenz. I was anxious to see how these cities appeared today and felt somewhat apprehensive as to what feelings the German people might harbor toward Americans and, particularly, toward those who participated in the bombing missions during World War II.

We were fortunate in having a native of Germany as our tour director who was a child during World War II, having lived in Hamburg at that time and now resided in Munich. She was fluent in seven languages including English and was able to provide much information from the perspective of a German civilian. There was also a member of our tour group, who is now a school teacher in Florida, who had spent her childhood in Germany and lived through the World War II bombings. Both she and our tour director related that the German people did not hate the Americans because they realized that the Americans were targeting industrial and military operations, not their cathedrals and other treasures of the country. They did harbor resentment toward the English because they felt their bombings were more indiscriminate and included so much that the German people held dear.

As we toured the cities, I could readily see why these particular cities were targets during the war and, surprisingly after all these years, evidence of those bombings still existed in many areas, particularly in Eastern Germany. Western Germany had done a great deal of rehabilitation. However, in East Berlin, bullet holes from the strafings were still apparent in some of the buildings. The over-all condition of the West was quite superior to that of the East. Check-Point Charley is now one of the tourist attractions as is the portion of the Berlin Wall still standing.

Our tour also included a visit to the American Cemetery at Luxembourg, which is not only beautiful but actually an emotional experience. The caretaker, upon learning that we were Americans, played a number of our patriotic songs in chimes over the chapel speakers that rang out over the cemetery. I believe every member of the tour was quite moved by this visit. From Luxembourg, we traveled on to the memorial at Bastogne, a truly magnificent tribute to all who fought so valiantly there.

We came home relieved that not only did the German people not appear to harbor resentment over the World War II experience, but truly seemed to welcome us and did what they could to ensure that we enjoyed our visit.

More Grandchildren

Our son, Jonathan, married Danielle Burbey on September 19, 1998, and acquired two daughters in the process, Savannah, born June 7, 1993, and Kaelyn born September 30, 1994. Then on the 25th of February 1999, they presented us with another grandson, Logan Jonathan Pace. Now I have a grandson to carry on the Pace name, which pleased me greatly. Olivia Marie Pace was born on May 4, 2001.

Visit to England and the Old Base

In May of 1999, my wife and I made a return trip to the Snetterton Heath Base site while on a tour of England, Scotland, Ireland and Wales. Geoff Ward, our English liaison with the 8th Air Force Historical Society, met us at Diss Station in Norwich and took us out to see what was still there. Having grown up in the area during the time we were stationed there, he has vivid memories of watching our planes taking off and various activities connected with the base. He, with the assistance of others, has established a museum on the site. He took us first to St. Andrews church at Quidenham where we saw the original 96th Bomb Group Memorial stained glass window. The church is about a thousand years old with beautiful stained glass windows. Then it was on to a tour of the former base. He pointed out where various units and buildings were located. There are some cement slabs where the planes were parked, some evidence of building locations and, actually, some buildings still standing and in use. Parts of the runways remain, and one portion is now a motorcycle race track. It was a nostalgic visit with the trees at the end of the runway still there and various buildings still on the grounds with many now being used for commercial purposes. A train came through on the tracks at Eccles Road just as it did, oh, so many years ago, and the man at the gate had to go out and put the crossing gates in place. The museum, our last stop on the visit, houses a vault of priceless information of great use to anyone interested in the history of this section of the war. The building itself is a Nissen hut that had formerly housed the ambulances and mortuary on the base.

QUIDENHAM

The Reading Room & Post Office
The village sign depicts Boadicea who
is reputed to be buried near the church.

St. Andrew's Church

Early 12th century North door

Late 13th century South door

St. Andrew's Church has a round tower
dating from 950-1050 A.D. with a 14th
century octagon top and a shingled spire.
The nave is mainly 13th & 14th century
and in the church there are many other
interesting features.

St. Andrew's window

Church Gate

The American Memorial Chapel
Dedicated by their colleagues to those servicemen
of the U.S.A.A.F. 96th Bomb Group who were
stationed at nearby Snetterton Heath
and who lost their lives 1943-1945.

Designed By Countryside Art Swbc Alfred Lion

St. Andrews Church at Quidenham

83

The 96th Bomb Group Memorial Chapel
St. Andrew's Church
Quidenham, Norfolk, England

The memorial depicts an American airman in flight clothes looking up at a figure of Christ with welcoming arms. Above, there is a formation of aircraft; below is the Spire of St. Andrew's Church over which the 96th assembled

The design also incorporates the emblems of the 8th Air Force, the 96th Bomb Group and those of the 96th's four squadrons.

Captain Herbert Allen, 338th flight surgeon, first promoted the idea for the memorial in April of 1944. With cooperation from his Squadron Executive Officer, Captain Robert L. Robb, the 96th Chaplain, Captain Charles Smith and Reverend Harper-Mitchell the wonderful Anglo-American project was underway.

The original design for the stained glass window was submitted by Sergeant Gerald Athey, 413th and sent to the architect, Mr. Reginald Bell. Mr. Bell's final design made only minimal changes that were dictated by ecclesiastical custom or by the constraints imposed by stained glass as a medium

Estimates were prepared and cost were projected at 597 Pounds. This amount exceeded the amount of non-essential construction permitted by the British wartime economy, and since the project would represent a permanent change to an existing historical landmark, permission was also required from higher levels of the Church. Group Adjutant, Colonel Moffett obtained the government's consent and the Chancellor's Court of the Church Of England granted a wavier for the project

A fund-raising campaign was held on the airbase. The money for the project was raised in two days.

The memorial stands today as an everlasting tribute to the 96ers who gave their lives, their fortunes and sacred honor in the fight for freedom.

Photo by Dale Budde 2001

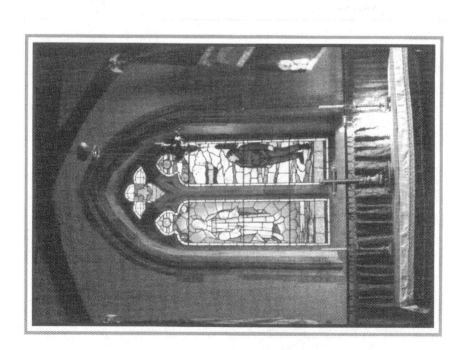

The 96ᵗʰ Bomb Group Memorial Chapel

The Silver Dream

Our Fortress flies again at Snetterton Heath, Station 138, The Falcons' Nest.

At the very top is a B-17 climbing away on a mission. Supporting the B-17 are four columns, representing contrails coming back from the engines. Those four columns increase in size as they reach the ground and are representative of the support needed to put the B-17 up there. Each column represents one of the four squadrons comprising the 96th Bomb Group.

The Memorial at Snetterton Heath as designed by Martin Rance is constructed of stainless steel by Sinclair Steel Fabrications and is located along the old North South runway now serving as the entrance road to the Octagon Motorsports racing circuit track

The plinth is inscribed as follows:

337TH

338TH

339TH

413TH

DEDICATED TO ALL PERSONNEL,
OF THE
96TH BOMBARDMENT GROUP (H)
8TH U.S.A.A.F.
WHO SERVED ON
THIS AIRFIELD
1943 - 1945

Photo by Bruce Martin 2003

The Silver Dream

I Get to Fly in a B-17 Again

I finally got to fly in a Flying Fortress, B-17, again on May 4, 2001 (same day our youngest granddaughter, Olivia Marie Pace, was born). The Arizona wing of the Confederate Air Force, a patriotic organization dedicated to the preservation of the world's great combat aircraft, comes to Gillespie Field in El Cajon, California, every year at this time and displays many old and some new aircraft. They also offer rides in one of the few remaining operational B-17s, the "Sentimental Journey", for a price. Knowing how I'd love to go up in a B-17 again, my wife insisted that I take the flight, and it truly was a sentimental journey for me. Having talked with those in charge and letting them know that I was a veteran of WWII and had flown in the B-17s as radio operator/gunner, they allowed me to begin our flight in my old position at the radio operator's desk. What an experience! I had forgotten how noisy these planes were! While in flight, the six of us participating in the flight changed places every ten minutes of the 30-minute flight allowing us to experience the flight in the various locations. I can't begin to describe the emotions I felt during that 30 minutes. It was still an awesome journey after 56+ years.

During the summer of 2007 I was treated to another B-17 flight at Gillespie Field when the "Liberty Belle" was brought in for viewing and rides. I had taken two of my grandchildren, Chris and Pamela Ward, ages 16 and 10 at the time, out to see the plane.

And the kind people there offered me a free ride as a token of appreciation for the part I played in World War II. Well, I certainly wasn't about to pass up this opportunity. It was just as exciting as the one back in 2001.

Joe Pace and "Liberty Belle" - 2007

GLOSSARY

5AD	5th Division British Royal Air Force
1AD	First Air Division British Royal Air Force
A/C	Aircraft
AFCE	Auto Pilot
B.A.R.	Browning Automatic Rifle
C.O.	Commanding Officer
FW-190	Fualkwulf German Fighter Aircraft
Tarmac Hard stand	A/C Parking Space
I.P.	Initial Point
K.P.	Kitchen Police
LNER	London Northeast Railroad
M.O.	Military Operation
MICROH	Pathfinder
M.P.I.	Main Point of Impact
ME-109	Messerschmitt Jet Fighter
M.P.	Military Police
P.F.C.	Private First Class
P.O.W.	Prisoner of War
P-51	Mustain Fighter Plane (U.S.)
R.A.F.	Royal Air Force
R&R	Rest and Recovery
R.T.U.	Reserve Training Unit